White Fang

Artists: Penko Gelev

Sotir Gelev

Editor: Stephen Haynes
Editorial Assistant: Mark Williams

Published in Great Britain in MMXI by
Book House, an imprint of
The Salariya Book Company Ltd
25 Marlborough Place, Brighton, BN1 1UB
www.salariya.com
www.book-house.co.uk

ISBN-13: 978-1-906714-74-1 (PB)

ṢALARIYA

© The Salariya Book Company Ltd MMXI

1 3 5 7 9 8 6 4 2

A CIP catalogue record for this book is available
from the British Library.

Printed and bound in China.
Printed on paper from sustainable sources.

Visit our website at **www.book-house.co.uk**
or go to **www.salariya.com** for **free** electronic versions of:
You Wouldn't Want to be an Egyptian Mummy!
You Wouldn't Want to be a Roman Gladiator!
You Wouldn't Want to be a Polar Explorer!
You Wouldn't Want to sail on a 19th-Century Whaling Ship!

Picture credits:
p. 40 ©2000 Topham Picturepoint/Topfoto.co.uk
p. 43 (Klondike map) Carolyn Franklin
p. 44 Bob Hersey
p. 47 Topfoto/HIP/Topfoto.co.uk; photographer Randal Kleiser

Every effort has been made to trace copyright holders. The Salariya Book Company apologises for any omissions and would be pleased, in such cases, to add an acknowledgement in future editions.

GRAFFEX

White Fang

Jack London

Illustrated by

Penko Gelev

Retold by

Tom Ratliff

BOOK HOUSE

Series created and designed by

David Salariya

The Klondike, Canada (Gold Rush country), in the late 1890s

Dark spruce forest frowned on either side of the frozen waterway. The trees seemed to lean towards each other, black and ominous, in the fading light. A vast silence reigned over the land – a desolation, lifeless, without movement. It was the Wild – the savage, frozen-hearted Northland Wild.

CHARACTERS

Kiche, the She-Wolf

Grey Beaver, a Native American trader

Weedon Scott, a mining engineer

Beauty Smith, a cook

Matt, in charge of Weedon Scott's dog team

Judge Scott, Weedon's father

White Fang

Bill and Henry, travellers in the Wild

Jim Hall, an escaped convict

THE TRAIL OF DEATH

Even in this dead land there is life, abroad and defiant...

...two men who are not yet dead – and a third whom the Wild has conquered.[1]

They're after us, Bill.

Meat is scarce — ain't seen a rabbit for days.

There are other living things in the frozen waste – predators driven by desperation and hunger.

The dogs are stayin' close to camp.

They'd sooner eat grub than *be* grub.

While Henry and Bill set up camp, the sled dogs cluster around the fire.

How many dogs we got?

Six.

Well, I had six fish and One-Ear didn't get one.

You counted wrong — or you're seein' things.

But when Bill feeds the dogs their supper, something is awry.

No, there's tracks in the snow — I'll show you.

Then you're thinkin' as it was — one of *them*?[2]

A long wailing cry pierces the darkness.

Think he minds us using his coffin for a table?

At least he don't have to worry about the wolves.

As the wolves press closer, the sled dogs panic.

We're almost out of ammunition.

I wish we was sittin' by the fire at Fort McGurry playing cribbage.[3]

Wolves got him — probably swallowed him alive.

In the morning one of the dogs, Fatty, is missing.

1. a third whom the Wild has conquered: The two men are travelling with the body of their companion who has died in the frozen wilderness.   2. one of *them*: Bill has accidentally given one of the fish to a wolf, mistaking it for a dog.
3. cribbage: a card game.

7

THE SHE-WOLF

The men set off before daybreak, with the starving wolves in pursuit. As night falls, they stop to gather firewood.

Bill is startled to find a wolf among the dogs!

I gave it a good whack, but it got half a fish.

I wish they'd go away an' leave us alone.

They do get on the nerves horrible.

The next morning Bill can only find four dogs.

Now Frog's gone.

He was the strongest of the bunch. What'd make *him* run off?

Next day, Spanker has gone – only three dogs remain.

I guess he's cavortin' over the landscape in the bellies of twenty different wolves.

The mystery begins to unravel as a she-wolf appears in the distance.

She's big — and that red colour — must be part dog.

She's been luring our dogs out of camp!

You're half eaten if you give in!

They're like sharks following a ship!

With only three dogs, it is harder to keep ahead of the wolves.

She ain't gonna get One-Ear!

She's gone!

When the sled overturns, Henry has to unhitch the dogs, and the She-Wolf claims another victim.

She knows a shootin' iron when she sees one.

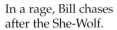

In a rage, Bill chases after the She-Wolf.

Now she's lured old Bill out too.

Only had three cartridges, Bill. Hope you made 'em count.

Henry listens to the snarls and yelps of a struggle whose outcome he knows.

Henry builds a scaffold to protect the dead man from the hungry wolves.

They got Bill an' they may get me, but they won't get you.

Without the coffin, Henry is able to outrun the wolves for a while.

Gotta stop soon and build the biggest fire I can.

Henry struggles to stay awake as the wolves slowly close in on his little camp.

If I doze, I'm a dead man for sure.

Get away, you devil!

As Henry nods off he is roused by an enormous grey wolf only a few feet away.

You can come and get me any time — I'm going to sleep.

Driven by hunger, the wolves close in for the kill. Henry has finally given up hope.

But fate intervenes, and the Wild is pierced with the cries of men, the churn of sleds and the creak of dog harnesses.

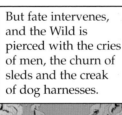

Where's Lord Alfred?

Roostin' in a tree just up river aways.

Dead?

An' in a box.

The red She-Wolf... she ate the dog food, then the dogs — and then she ate Bill.

THE BATTLE OF THE FANGS

With the She-Wolf at the head of the pack, the wolves begin their search for food again.

They come upon a quarry who is no match for twenty sets of fangs.

As the mating season approaches, the pack begins to break up. Three suitors[1] vie for the She-Wolf.

The youngest is quickly defeated by the more experienced fighters.

Then old One-Eye lashes out at the Grey Leader, tearing his throat open.

One-Eye and the She-Wolf hunt together, stealing food from an Indian snare.

Soon the She-Wolf is heavy with cubs. She finds a lair in a washed-out cave.

Now she must rely on One-Eye to bring her food.

Even the wolves have enemies in the Northland, and when One-Eye encounters a lynx, he carefully avoids confronting this deadly foe.

1. suitors: males in search of a mate.

One morning One-Eye is awakened by the whimpering of five feeble, helpless little bundles of life.

Four of the cubs have the reddish hue of their mother but one has the grey fur of his father.

The grey cub is longer and leaner than his brothers and sisters, and his rasping growl is the loudest.

The cubs soon outgrow their mother's milk, and need meat to survive.

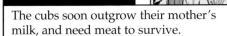

One-Eye struggles to find enough meat to keep his young cubs from starving.

Only the strongest will survive, and the old wolf is no match for the sharp claws of a hungry lynx.

Now the She-Wolf is forced to leave her cubs and hunt.

Only the grey cub is tough enough to survive the famine.

THE WALL OF LIGHT

With his mother away hunting, the grey cub is left alone to explore his world.

Though he is curious, the cub does not cross the wall of light at the mouth of the cave.

The instincts[1] of a thousand thousand ancestors warn him of the danger.

He senses danger even before he sees the hungry wolverine.[2]

But one day his hunger and curiosity get the better of him.

Blinded by the brightness of the outside world, he tumbles down the riverbank.

Some animals are beyond his reach...

...but others are easy prey.

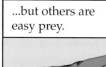

The cub enjoys the rewards of his first hunt.

1. instincts: skills or knowledge that an animal is born with, and does not have to learn.
2. wolverine: a fierce, badger-like carnivore related to the weasel.

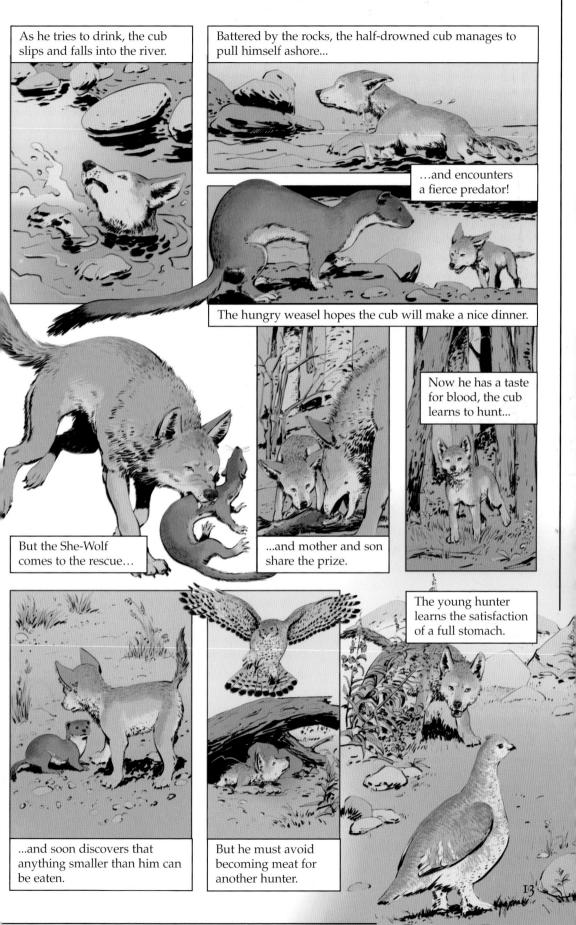

As he tries to drink, the cub slips and falls into the river.

Battered by the rocks, the half-drowned cub manages to pull himself ashore...

...and encounters a fierce predator!

The hungry weasel hopes the cub will make a nice dinner.

Now he has a taste for blood, the cub learns to hunt...

But the She-Wolf comes to the rescue...

...and mother and son share the prize.

The young hunter learns the satisfaction of a full stomach.

...and soon discovers that anything smaller than him can be eaten.

But he must avoid becoming meat for another hunter.

KICHE

One day the cub discovers another kind of hunter.

As the She-Wolf comes to the rescue of her cub, one of the Indians recognises her.

The She-Wolf submits to the hand of Grey Beaver.

He is three-quarters wolf, this son of Kiche. I shall call him White Fang.

The village children are excited to see the new pup.

But the dogs are not so welcoming, and the cub has to be rescued by Grey Beaver.

The largest pup, Lip-lip, torments White Fang. The grey cub must learn to defend himself.

He is curious to learn about the godlike creatures who live in the village.

Fascinated by a campfire, he burns his nose. Yet what hurts worse is the laughter of men.

Ha!

YELP!

Chewed and cut by Lip-lip, the grey cub is unsubdued.[1]

Targeted by the other dogs, White Fang never barks, in joy or anger. His silence marks him out even more.

Not allowed to share the other dogs' food, he must rely on his hunting instincts, becoming a thief to stay alive.

Craftily the grey cub lures Lip-lip away from the pack.

Once they are away from the village, White Fang suddenly attacks his tormentor.

He's becoming a strong fighter...

...but occasionally Grey Beaver has to come to the rescue.

1. is unsubdued: refuses to give in.

HIS FIRST MASTER

Father, can she be trusted?

She will not wander far, Mit-sah.

Eventually, Grey Beaver allows Kiche to roam free.

White Fang is overjoyed. His instinct for the Wild revives, yet Kiche is content to stay near the village.

Three Eagles, a visiting trader, brings cloth, skins and rifle cartridges.

In return, Three Eagles takes Kiche. He prepares to leave with his new dog.

Terrified of losing his mother, White Fang dives into the river and swims after the trader's canoe.

But Grey Beaver easily retrieves his property...

When White Fang lashes out, the beating becomes more severe.

He is learning that he must obey Grey Beaver...

...and teaches the cub a lesson.

He has violated the most important law of the gods[1] – never fight back.

...yet his instincts are still strong, and the loss of his mother hangs heavily.

1. the gods: This is how White Fang thinks of humans.

White Fang is a skilled hunter and fighter. Soon many camp dogs bear the scars of his fangs.

He becomes an outcast, hated by man and dog alike.

He learns to protect himself in a fight, and to use surprise to his advantage.

He learns to knock his enemy to the ground, exposing the soft throat.

He becomes more vicious, eventually killing a larger dog by slashing its throat.

While the Indians prepare for the autumn hunt, White Fang hides in the woods, determined to stay behind.

But as night falls, he becomes cold and hungry. He misses Grey Beaver and the warmth of the fire.

He runs all day without rest, and finally comes upon fresh tracks in the newly fallen snow. He expects a beating...

...but Grey Beaver is happy to see the wolf-dog, and gladly shares his supper with him.

THE COVENANT[1]

Grey Beaver is going up river to trade.

His son Mit-sah rides a smaller sled –

– with White Fang in his team.

Lip-lip, as leader, gets special treatment, which makes the other dogs jealous.

White Fang despises him.

White Fang never misses an opportunity to steal food. He is a monstrous tyrant[2] to the weaker dogs.

Finally they reach a large village on the shores of the Great Slave Lake.

One of the villagers tries to steal from Grey Beaver.

White Fang lashes out at the thief.

Grey Beaver will not let the angry villagers harm his dog.

When Mit-sah is attacked by some village boys, White Fang chases the attackers away.

There are rewards for protecting Grey Beaver and his family –

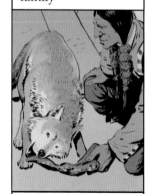

– but White Fang serves them out of duty, not love.

1. covenant: a solemn agreement about how one person or group of people should treat another.
2. tyrant: cruel oppressor; bully.

In spring, Grey Beaver returns home. White Fang is now a year old.

His body is slender and rangy, his coat a true wolf-grey.

He is ready to fight all who dare cross him.

But the law of the Wild protects females, and when a mother dog snarls at him, White Fang backs down.

That summer, food is scarce. In the village, women and children go without.

While ordinary dogs starve, White Fang hunts to stay alive. He learns to fight weasels, and even lynx.

It's his own mother, but she does not remember him.

Attacked by a pack of wolves, White Fang outruns them...

When he meets Lip-lip out hunting, he kills his hated rival.

Returning to Grey Beaver's camp, he is rewarded with a fish.

...and eventually circles back to kill and eat one of his pursuers.

I see that the wolf-dog has survived the starving time.

A New Master

White Fang and Grey Beaver set out across the Rocky Mountains.

In every village, White Fang is attacked by other dogs.

The outcome is always the same.

They travel downriver to Fort Yukon. Men from the Southland stop here on their way to the goldfields of the Klondike.

Grey Beaver sells furs, mittens and moccasins[1] to the Southlanders.

White Fang distrusts the white men and snarls if they try to touch him.

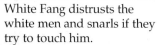

The white men's dogs hate the wolf...

...but he makes quick work of them.

Some of the men set their dogs on him just for fun.

1. moccasins: traditional Native American shoes made of soft leather.

One man enjoys the violence so much that he sometimes leaps into the air with delight.

He's a cruel coward, trusted by no-one. Men jokingly call him Beauty Smith.

He wants to buy Grey Beaver's fighting dog.

Dog not for sale.

Well, take a bottle of whisky and think about it, friend.

Grey Beaver develops a thirst for whisky. Soon his money is gone. The dog is all he has.

If you can catch him, he's yours.

But Beauty Smith cannot catch him without help.

Beauty Smith beats the dog when he tries to escape.

After a second attempt, he thrashes him with a whip.

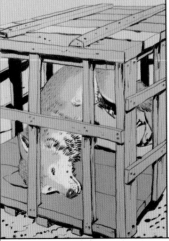

The third time, White Fang gets a beating that would have killed any other dog. Now he is chained in a strong cage.

THE REIGN OF HATE

Controlled by an evil and heartless man, White Fang becomes a ruthless fiend.

The laughter and the teasing are even worse than the daily beatings.

White Fang becomes the enemy of all things –

GRRR!

– willing to lash out at any creature.

A prize fight is arranged.

My money's on the mastiff.[1]

Nah, the wolf'll eat him alive.

In a few seconds White Fang rips the mastiff's throat open.

Beauty Smith laughs with glee as he collects his winnings.

I'm gonna be rich!

'The Fighting Wolf' becomes the main attraction at the fort.

Beauty Smith even makes White Fang take on two dogs at once, but the result is the same.

22   1. mastiff: a large, muscular breed of dog.

Beauty takes 'The Fighting Wolf' to Dawson City.

All the passengers want to see the savage beast – the most ferocious killer in the Wild.

In Dawson, he is displayed in a cage. Someone pokes him to frighten the crowd.

But White Fang resists all attempts to break his spirit.

Dog fighting is illegal in Dawson, so Beauty Smith has to stage his fights in the woods outside the town.

Driven to near madness by Beauty Smith, White Fang unleashes his fury against his opponents, and none can withstand him.

He's a killer, that one.

He never loses his footing.

Finally, Beauty Smith brings in a wild lynx.

This fight lasts longer, but ends with White Fang victorious again.

White Fang takes on all comers – hounds, malamutes,[1] Eskimo dogs, Labradors – but he is too fast and too powerful for all of them.

1. malamutes: Alaskan sled dogs.

THE CLINGING DEATH

A new challenger arrives in town.

The wolf'll make short work of him.

Go to him, Cherokee!

Instead of attacking, the bulldog stares at the crowd cheering him on.

Sic'm,[1] Cherokee! Eat'm up!

Nah, them bulldog jaws is powerful.

Cherokee is too low to knock over, and has no loose fur to grab hold of.

His massive jaws protect the soft underside of his neck.

Both dogs are cut and bruised, but neither can get the upper hand.

When White Fang loses his balance, Cherokee is at his throat.

I don't believe it!

White Fang cannot shake off the clinging bulldog.

Cherokee begins to push against the wolf, inching slowly for the jugular vein.[2]

Though a furious Beauty Smith tries to egg him on, White Fang is exhausted.

1. Sic'm: Attack him.
2. jugular vein: a major vein in the throat; if the bulldog bites through it, White Fang will bleed to death.

The crowd becomes uneasy when two men arrive. They think it's a police raid to break up the dog fight.

It's Weedon Scott, a mining expert, and his dog-musher,[1] Matt.

What's going on here?

You cowards! You beasts!

As Weedon Scott tries to pull the dogs apart, the crowd jeers.

No use, Mr Scott, can't break 'em apart that way.

Using the barrel of his revolver, Matt tries to prise the bulldog's jaws open.

Don't break them teeth, mister

Can you help us?

Slowly the bulldog's jaws begin to open.

Sorry, I don't know how.

Then get out of the way.

If the bulldog bites through the jugular, this one's a goner.

How much is a good sled dog worth?

Three hundred dollars.

How much for one that's chewed up like this?

Did you hear that, Mr Beast? I'm going to give you a hundred and fifty for him.

A man's got his rights, you know.

You're no man. You're a beast.

I ain't gonna sell.

Half that.

White Fang is barely breathing.

1. dog-musher: a trainer and driver of dog-sled teams.

THE INDOMITABLE[1]

He's a wolf. There'll be no taming him.

Wolf or dog, he's been trained, broke to the harness. Look at the marks across his chest.

Will he ever be a sled dog again?

Not likely — he's a killer now.

The poor devil needs some human kindness.

I guess it's hopeless.

He's been through hell — give'm time.

As Weedon Scott approaches, the wolf strikes.

GRRRRR!

It would be a mercy to kill him.

Let's let him run loose first, and see what happens.

What are you doing?

It's the right thing to do.

Put up the gun.

This dog is too intelligent to kill

White Fang is familiar with rifles and cowers in fear.

As Matt puts down the gun, the dog becomes calm.

1. indomitable: unable to be tamed or made to submit.

Weedon Scott begins his reclamation of the wolf-dog. He sits several feet away, talking softly.

When Scott offers fresh meat, the wolf-dog holds back, waiting to see what the man will do.

Weedon Scott tosses him the meat and moves a little closer.

When the meat is gone, Scott reaches out his hand and gently touches the wolf-dog's neck.

GRRRR!

Well, I'll be gosh-swoggled!

You're seventeen kinds of fool and all of'm different.

Puzzled by the man's kindness, White Fang allows Scott to caress him again.

Patiently, Weedon Scott wins the wolf-dog's trust.

But is it possible to redeem the heart of a killer wolf who has never known kindness?

LOVE AND TRUST

Only the love of a special person can save White Fang.

White Fang explores his new home.

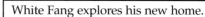

He learns to tolerate those who mean no harm.

Weedon Scott makes a point of caressing the dog often.

When Scott goes off to town, White Fang sits for hours waiting for him – though he never barks or shows joy when Scott returns.

He learns to leave his master's dogs alone, and tolerates Matt – but only because Matt feeds him.

He even allows himself to be harnessed to work with the other dogs, just to please his new master.

When you took this dog, you clean swindled Beauty Smith.

The beast!

But he knows that his primary duty is to guard his master's property.

When Weedon Scott has to go away on business, White Fang begins to pine. Matt writes to his employer.

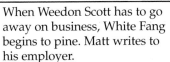

That wolf won't eat. Don't even fight the other dogs. Mebbe[1] he is going to die.

When Scott returns, White Fang wags his tail and growls with happiness.

I always knew this wolf was a dog.

Listen to him singing!

GRRR

The Wild has taught White Fang defiance, but now he learns to sing and snuggle.

Wolf's nailed somebody.

AAARGH!

One night, as the men play cribbage, a cry of anguish fills the air.

White Fang has recognised the intruder, and ripped his arms and legs to shreds.

Come on, boy. Whoever he is, he's had enough.

Better get going before we let the wolf loose on ya again.

Must'a' thought he had hold of seventeen devils.

The beast!

That devil tried to steal you, eh? He made a mistake, didn't he?

It's Beauty Smith, trying to get his dog back.

1. Mebbe: Maybe (this is Matt's own spelling).

THE LONG TRAIL

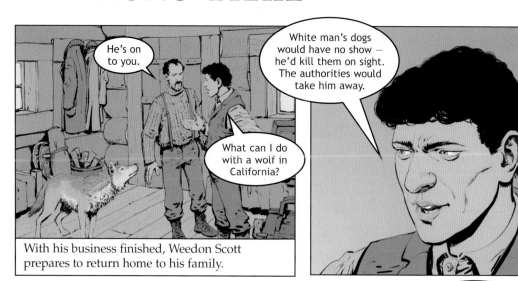

"He's on to you."

"White man's dogs would have no show — he'd kill them on sight. The authorities would take him away."

"What can I do with a wolf in California?"

With his business finished, Weedon Scott prepares to return home to his family.

"He's a downright murderer."

"I'd have to hire someone to take care of him."

White Fang knows something is up – a change he will not be allowed to share.

"No denying he thinks a lot of you."

"Shut up — I know what's best."

"I'm agreein' with you, only..."

"Only what?"

"One'd think you didn't know your own mind."

"You're right, Matt. I don't know."

"It would be rank ridiculousness to take that dog along."

"I agree. But how in the great Sardanapolis[1] he knows you're goin' is what gets me."

1. the great Sardanapolis: Jack London may have heard this quaint expression on his travels; Sardanapalus was an ancient Assyrian king.

White Fang is silent, but snuggles in Scott's arms.

Locked in the cabin, the dog begins a heart-breaking howl.

The *Aurora* is jammed with prosperous and broken adventurers, all mad to get to the Outside[1]...

...and waiting on the deck is White Fang!

1. the Outside: the world outside the Klondike.

THE SOUTHLAND

The long ocean voyage is followed by a short train ride. White Fang sleeps for much of the trip.

It is a happy reunion for Weedon as his wife and parents welcome him home.

Is that a wolf?

It's OK, Alice — he's just protecting me.

The Scotts head for home with White Fang in tow.

At the family home, Sierra Vista, they are met by Collie the sheepdog.

Here, Collie.

Collie rushes the intruder. White Fang cannot attack a female, so he runs away.

A deerhound named Dick attacks. Collie saves the hound's life by knocking the wolf over.

This is a pretty warm reception for a poor lone wolf from the Arctic.

White Fang has only been knocked down once before in his life.

Let's let Dick and the wolf fight it out. They'll become friends soon enough.

Dick wouldn't stand a chance.

Judge Scott, Weedon's father, doesn't realise the danger.

White Fang grows to love his new home. Life is easy.

Dick tries to be friendly, but White Fang snarls at him.

Collie picks on him whenever she can. He does his best to ignore her.

Although distrustful of most people, he guards those who are dear to his master.

The wolf-dog is soon a member of the family, though only the master receives his special love-growl.

A stern word from the master is all it takes to teach White Fang how to behave.

THE WOLF-DOG

But he is a still a wolf...

He kills a chicken, and attacks the groom who tries to punish him. Collie comes to the rescue.

Two nights later White Fang jumps into the chicken coop and kills fifty chickens.

The master scolds him, then leaves him alone in the chicken yard. There are no more killings.

But when Dick chases a jackrabbit,[1] White Fang is allowed to join in.

On trips into town he must cope with cats and dogs and crowded sidewalks.

When attacked by other dogs, he learns not to fight back...

...until one day, Weedon Scott decides he's had enough.

Go for it! Eat them up!

At his master's word, White Fang leaps silently at his attackers and the dust rises like a cloud.

Soon the word in the Santa Clara Valley is not to mess with the Fighting Wolf.

1. jackrabbit: an American hare.

Treated with human kindness, White Fang flourishes like a flower planted in good soil.

Yet the Wild still lingers in him...

Most other dogs growl at his approach. But a snarl is enough to keep them at a safe distance.

But Collie's sharp and nervous snarl is ever in his ears.

Lying down and pretending to sleep does not deter her.

He shows affection for only one living thing.

White Fang has never played with other dogs.

Now he learns to romp and play-fight with his master.

He loves to run alongside when his master goes riding.

One day a jackrabbit startles the master's horse.

It's a nasty spill, and Weedon Scott knows his leg is broken!

THE TAME WOLF

Weedon Scott is in so much pain he can't move. His only hope is the dog.

At first everyone thinks Weedon has returned early, and cannot understand why White Fang is agitated.

White Fang tugs at Alice's dress, which frightens her.

After this, White Fang is loved by all at Sierra Vista.

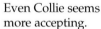

Even Collie seems more accepting.

One morning, White Fang doesn't come running when his master calls.

Instead, he and Collie run together as his mother and old One-Eye did years before.

A violent criminal has escaped from San Quentin prison.

No punishment could break Jim Hall's spirit.

When a cruel guard taunted him, Hall turned on the man and bit his throat.

He spent three years alone in an iron cage, growling like an animal when his food was delivered.

He killed four warders during his escape, and police for miles around are on the alert.

It was Judge Scott who sent Jim Hall to prison, and the convict had sworn revenge.

The man will be caught if he comes within ten miles of here.

News of Hall's escape brings anxiety to Sierra Vista, but the Judge stays calm.

Every night, Alice secretly lets White Fang into the house to sleep in the big hall.

One night he is woken by the scent of a stranger.

THE BLESSED WOLF

White Fang stalks the intruder silently, like the hunter he is.

Suddenly...

BAM!
BAM!

Sierra Vista awakes in alarm to the sound of pistol shots and battling fiends!

SMASH!

CRASH!

AAARGH!

In the midst of the wreckage lies a man.

It's Jim Hall. His throat's ripped out.

He's all in, poor devil.

We'll see about that.

He's lost most of his blood.

He hasn't a chance in ten thousand.

But he mustn't lose any chance. Never mind the expense. Put him under X-ray, anything.

If he survives the night, he must be nursed round the clock.

White Fang's injuries seem hopeless, but the Judge is determined to save him.

Weedon's sisters, Mary and Beth, take turns nursing the dog. It takes many weeks.

But the son of She-Wolf and One-Eye is strong, and clings to life.

He sleeps most of the time. In his dreams he revisits his past life.

He survived because he's a wolf.

A blessed wolf!

That shall be my name for him.

He needs fresh air and sunlight. Take him outside.

It is a gala day when his bandages are removed.

With each step, White Fang feels his strength returning.

In the stable Collie is lying with a litter of pups. Curious, he approaches, but she snarls, and he keeps his distance.

One tiny puppy approaches and their noses touch.

The Blessed Wolf lies contentedly with half-shut eyes, drowsing in the sun.

The end 39

JACK LONDON (1876–1916)

Jack London was an American author who wrote books and short stories that portrayed strong-willed men and women in their struggles against the forces of nature and human society. His best-known works, *The Call of the Wild* (1903) and *White Fang* (1906), are both set in the frozen reaches of the Klondike–Yukon wilderness (see pages 42–43) that London experienced first hand during the gold rush of the 1890s. Jack London was one of the most popular and highest-paid authors of his time, and his works have been translated into several languages and enjoyed by readers around the world.

Jack London in 1914

EARLY LIFE

Jack London was born in San Francisco, California. His mother, Flora Wellman, was abandoned by Jack's father (William Chaney), and when Jack was still a baby she married John London. The family moved to Oakland, California, where Jack grew up and attended school.

Bored with formal education, Jack dropped out in the eighth grade instead of going to high school. He sold newspapers on the street corner, and in quick succession worked in a laundry, a cannery and a jute mill. He briefly worked as an 'oyster pirate', stealing oysters at night from offshore oyster farms. Jack then signed on to the crew of a seal-hunting ship headed for Japan. He became an experienced sailor and developed a lifelong love of the sea, which he used as the setting for many of his stories, including *The Sea Wolf*, *The Mutiny of the Elsinore* and *South Sea Tales*.

Jack loved to read and spent long hours in the Oakland Public Library. Intent on continuing his education, he returned to school at 19 and received his high school diploma. He enrolled at the University of California at Berkeley, but dropped out after one term for financial reasons.

In 1897 Jack went north to pan for gold in the Klondike, where he suffered from scurvy and malnutrition. He established a reputation with the other prospectors as a storyteller, but was unsuccessful in his search for gold.

BECOMING A WRITER

The next year, Jack London returned to San Francisco, where he settled down to pursue a career in writing. His early success came when some of his short stories were published in *Overland Monthly* and *Atlantic Monthly* magazines. His first book, *The Son of the Wolf*, published in 1900, was a collection of his previously published stories.

In 1900 Jack married Bess Maddern. They had two daughters, but in 1905 London divorced Bess and eventually married Charmian Kittredge, a woman who was the model for several of his strong female characters.

Jack London was a prolific writer, producing 51 books, four plays, dozens of short stories, and numerous articles for newspapers and magazines – all in just 18 years. A disciplined writer, he found time to work every morning and usually produced at least a thousand words a day.

TRAPPINGS OF SUCCESS

In 1905 Jack purchased Beauty Ranch, a large property in the Valley of the Moon in Sonoma County, California. Here he raised a variety of animals including bulls, horses and pigs, and had a 40-acre (16-hectare) vineyard where he grew wine grapes. He befriended the famous botanist and plant specialist Luther Burbank, who helped him develop new crops to cultivate on Beauty Ranch.

In 1906 Jack London oversaw the construction of the *Snark*, a custom-built sailing ship. Jack and his wife Charmian spent two years on an extended voyage in the South Pacific, which provided material for several of his books and short stories.

Jack London was only 40 when he died of kidney failure on 22 November 1916. He is buried in Jack London State Park, in Glen Ellen, Sonoma County, California.

JACK LONDON WEB RESOURCES

The Jack London Online Collection: http://london.sonoma.edu/
Jack London Main Page: http://www.jacklondon.com/
The World of Jack London: http://www.jacklondons.net/
Biography and Works: http://www.online-literature.com/london/
Illustrated Biography: http://www.jacklondons.net/shortbio.html
Naturalism: http://www.eng.umu.se/culturec/NAT.htm

THE KLONDIKE GOLD RUSH

The Klondike, also known as the Yukon, is an area that encompasses parts of Alaska and Canada, and is named for the two main rivers of the region – the Yukon and the Klondike.

Gold was discovered near Dawson City, in the Yukon Territory of Canada, in August 1896, along a tributary of the Yukon River called Rabbit Creek (later renamed Bonanza Creek). Word of the discovery reached the United States in July 1897, creating a 'gold rush' as over 40,000 people flocked to the Northland in search of gold. Among these prospectors was Jack London.

The goldfields were in a remote area of the northern wilderness, hundreds of miles from the nearest town or settlement. To survive for a year in the harsh conditions of the Klondike, a man (few women made the journey) needed to carry in 'a ton' of gear and equipment, including several hundred pounds of food: flour, bacon, oats, beans, sugar, coffee, tea, canned fruits and soups, and dried potatoes. Prospectors also needed lots of warm clothing, as well as blankets, tents, guns and ammunition, a small stove, assorted dishes, pots and pans, cutlery – and, of course, tools for mining: picks, shovels, hammers, axes, a two-man saw and gold pans.

Most of the prospectors came from the United States or Canada, but men from all over the world flocked to the Northland in search of gold. There were three routes favored by the prospectors. All started with an ocean-going steamer, with destinations either at the southern Alaska port towns of Skagway or Dyea (pronounced 'die-EE'), or a more northerly route that landed you near the mouth of the Yukon River at St Michael, Alaska. Wherever they landed, however, the miners still faced an arduous overland trek to reach the goldfields several hundred miles inland.

About 20 per cent of the gold seekers sailed north to St Michael and hiked up the Yukon River, avoiding the mountains that the southern routes entailed. From Skagway, prospectors faced a difficult journey over the White Pass Trail, while those who landed at Dyea had to cross the Coast Mountains over the 33-mile (53-km) Chilkoot Trail that included a rugged and difficult climb over the 3,500-foot (1,070-metre) Chilkoot Pass. All three routes were hazardous, and just getting to the goldfields proved to be too much for some of the men. It took a great deal of stamina, courage and determination to survive the ordeal of living in the frozen Northland, and only a very lucky few ever found the riches they sought.

KLONDIKE WEB RESOURCES

Gold Rush: http://www.postalmuseum.si.edu/gold/gold2.html
National Historic Park: http://www.nps.gov/klgo/index.htm
Photo Essay: http://www.ralphmag.org/DO/klondike.html
Wolves: http://www.wolfsongalaska.org/wolf_folklore.html

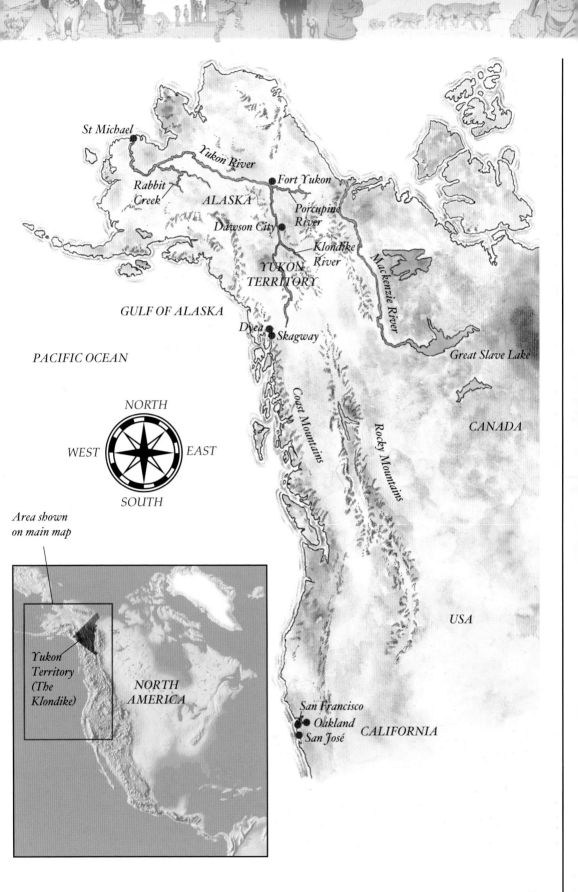

St Michael

Yukon River

Rabbit
Creek

Fort Yukon

ALASKA

Porcupine
River

Dawson City

Klondike
River

YUKON
TERRITORY

Mackenzie River

GULF OF ALASKA

Dyea

Skagway

Great Slave Lake

PACIFIC OCEAN

NORTH

WEST   EAST

SOUTH

Coast Mountains

Rocky Mountains

CANADA

USA

Area shown
on main map

Yukon
Territory
(The
Klondike)

NORTH
AMERICA

San Francisco

Oakland

San José

CALIFORNIA

DOGS AND WOLVES

Dogs have been used as working animals for thousands of years, and have assisted people in hunting and herding as well as serving to protect villages and farms from intruders. In the northern climates dogs were often used as pack animals and have been trained to pull sleds, singly or in teams. Several breeds have been used as sled dogs, although the most common are the Alaskan malamute, the Canadian Eskimo dog and the Siberian husky. Although any medium-sized dog can be trained to pull a sled, the best animals are those that show extraordinary speed and endurance.

The grey wolf (*Canis lupus*) belongs to the same genus (group of species) as coyotes, jackals and domestic dogs. Wolves once inhabited much of Eurasia and North America but were hunted to near extinction, and today are found only in remote areas. The wolf is an apex predator, which means that it has no natural enemies (except man), and sits at the top of the food chain. Wolves are territorial and usually hunt in packs, although during late winter and early spring the packs disperse as the animals pair off for mating.

Wolves attack their prey in one of two ways: by striking at the back legs near the hips (in order to knock the animal down) or by slashing at the victim's throat (which produces a quick death if the jugular vein is punctured). Therefore, the best defence against a wolf is for the prey to stay on its feet and keep its head down.

Wolves are easily tamed when they are young, and, though many countries have laws against owning the animals, wolves have been used as pets as well as working dogs for many hundreds of years. Folklore is filled with tales of wolves preying on people, but the animals are usually afraid of man and will only attack if provoked, or in rare cases during times of famine.

In fairytales such as *Little Red Riding Hood* or *The Three Little Pigs*, the wolf is always the villain. But in some cultures, legends and stories portray wolves as intelligent, helpful and wise – even heroic. Well-known examples are the wolves who adopt Mowgli in Kipling's *Jungle Book*, and the ancient Roman legend of Romulus and Remus, the founders of Rome, who were said to have been brought up by a she-wolf.

Grey wolf

Husky

44

REALISM AND NATURALISM

In America after the Civil War (1861–1865), two new styles of writing emerged: Realism, which sought to portray the everyday lives of average people; and Naturalism, which presented people as products of their environment or of the forces of nature. Realism and Naturalism were very different from the earlier Romantic style, which focused on heroic characters and ideals (and the idea that people could be improved by art), and from Sentimentalism, which dealt with questions of morality as well as human feelings and emotions.

American Realists include Henry James and Mark Twain, while the Naturalists are embodied in the work of Stephen Crane and Frank Norris. Many of these authors present women as strong central characters. While some stories of this type have happy endings, others see the main character dying a lonely or miserable death.

The writings of Charles Darwin and Herbert Spencer had a great influence on authors of this period in Europe and the United States. Darwin proposed the theory of evolution, while Spencer invented the phrase 'survival of the fittest'. Many books and short stories written between 1860 and 1914 reflect the theme of survival.

Jack London's works, including *White Fang*, have Naturalist themes, such as the indifference of nature, the struggle for survival, the inability of the characters to rise above their nature or upbringing (or to exercise free will), and the inner passions (lust, greed, a desire for power or dominance) that exist in all creatures.

In the United States, Realism and Naturalism were seen as reflecting the democratic character of American life, and many authors created stories about the powerless in American society: working men and women, minorities, or immigrants seeking to survive or succeed in a world that discriminated against them. Naturalism especially focused on the darker side of life, addressing the themes of poverty, alcoholism, prostitution, racism, disease and squalor. Many Realist or Naturalist authors hoped to improve conditions for women, minorities and working-class people through their writings.

WHITE FANG WEB RESOURCES

Text: http://london.sonoma.edu/Writings/WhiteFang/
Gutenberg: http://www.gutenberg.org/ebooks/910
ReadPrint: http://www.readprint.com/work-1010/White-Fang-Jack-London

JACK LONDON'S MAJOR WORKS

1900: *The Son of the Wolf*. Nine Klondike stories previously published in magazines.

1901: *The God of His Fathers*. A second series of short stories.

1902: *A Daughter of the Snows*. His first novel.

1902: *The Cruise of the Dazzler*. Escapades of the 'Frisco Kid'.

1903: *The Kempton–Wace Letters*. A novel in letters, co-written with Anna Strunsky.

1903: *The Call of the Wild*. The story of Buck, a sled dog, who returns to live in the wild.

1903: *People of the Abyss*. A non-fiction work about the slums of London.

1904: *The Sea-Wolf*. Chronicles of the fictional Wolf Larsen.

1904: *The Faith of Men and Other Stories*. A third collection of Northland stories.

1906: *White Fang*.

1906: *Before Adam*. A story about time travel to a prehistoric world.

1906: *Moon Face*. Short-story collection.

1907: *The Iron Heel*. A futuristic story of socialist revolution.

1910: *Burning Daylight*. A tale of the Klondike gold rush that criticises capitalist society.

1910: *Revolution and Other Essays*. Stories and writings that express London's political ideals.

1910: *To Build a Fire*. A short story of hardship and survival, set in the Klondike.

1911: *Adventure*. A story of slavery on a copra plantation in the Solomon Islands.

1911: *The Cruise of the Snark*. The autobiographical story of London's Pacific voyage of 1907–1908.

1911: *South Sea Tales*. Short stories set in the South Pacific.

1912: *The Scarlet Plague*. Futuristic novella about a plague that wipes out most of humanity.

1913: *John Barleycorn*. A story of the ravages of alcohol that some scholars believe is an autobiographical study of London's own alcoholism.

1913: *Martin Eden*. A semi-autobiographical novel.

1913: *The Valley of the Moon*. Working-class struggles in California's cities.

1914: *The Mutiny on the Elsinore*. A story of the struggle for survival during a mutiny.

1914: *The Star Rover*. A novel exposing the horrors of torture at San Quentin prison.

1916: *The Acorn Planter*. A play about a fictional Native American tribe's first encounters with Europeans.

1916: *The Little Lady of the Big House*. A triangular romance set in the California farm country.

1916: *Stories of Hawaii* – also known as *Tales of the Pacific*.

1917: *Michael, Brother of Jerry*. A story about animal cruelty that led to the formation of animal welfare leagues, known as Jack London Clubs.

JACK LONDON ON FILM

Jack London's adventure stories have inspired movie makers since they were first published in the early 1900s. D. W. Griffith and other early movie directors were fascinated with London's writings and made use of his exciting backdrops in creating some of the earliest action films. Jack London even appeared in *The Sea-Wolf*, playing the part of a sailor. Here are some of the best-loved versions of *White Fang*:

1925: *White Fang*, silent film directed by Laurence Trimble.

1936: *White Fang*, black and white film starring John Carradine as Beauty Smith.

1946: *Belyy Klyk* (*White Fang*), Finnish adaptation of London's story.

1973: *Zanna Bianca* (*White Fang*), Italian film starring Franco Nero as Jason Scott.

1974: *White Fang to the Rescue*, Italian film directed by Tonino Ricci.

1974: *Il Ritorno di Zanna Bianca* (*The Return of White Fang* or *The Challenge of White Fang*), directed by Lucio Fulci.

1974: *La Spacconata* (*White Fang and the Gold Diggers*), directed by Alfonso Brescia.

1975: *Zanna Bianca e il Cacciatore Solitario* (*White Fang and the Hunter*), directed by Alfonso Brescia.

1991: *White Fang*, Walt Disney Studios.

1993–1994: *White Fang*, television series starring Ken Blackburn.

1994: *White Fang 2: Myth of the White Wolf*, directed by Ken Olin.

1997: *White Fang*, animated version directed by Michael Sporn.

Klaus Maria Brandauer as Alex Larson and Jed as White Fang, in the 1991 film loosely based on Jack London's novel.

INDEX

IF YOU ENJOYED THIS BOOK, YOU MIGHT LIKE TO TRY THESE OTHER GRAFFEX TITLES:

Adventures of Huckleberry Finn Mark Twain

Beowulf

Dr Jekyll and Mr Hyde Robert Louis Stevenson

Dracula Bram Stoker

Frankenstein Mary Shelley

Gulliver's Travels Jonathan Swift

Hamlet William Shakespeare

The Hunchback of Notre Dame Victor Hugo

Jane Eyre Charlotte Brontë

Journey to the Centre of the Earth Jules Verne

Julius Caesar William Shakespeare

Kidnapped Robert Louis Stevenson

The Last of the Mohicans James Fenimore Cooper

Macbeth William Shakespeare

The Man in the Iron Mask Alexandre Dumas

The Merchant of Venice William Shakespeare

A Midsummer Night's Dream William Shakespeare

Moby-Dick Herman Melville

The Odyssey Homer

Oliver Twist Charles Dickens

Robinson Crusoe Daniel Defoe

Romeo and Juliet William Shakespeare

A Tale of Two Cities Charles Dickens

The Three Musketeers Alexandre Dumas

Treasure Island Robert Louis Stevenson

Twenty Thousand Leagues Under the Sea Jules Verne

Wuthering Heights Emily Brontë